Malcontent

Z D Dicks

Black Eyes Publishing UK

Malcontent
By Z D Dicks
© Z D Dicks 2019

Published by Black Eyes Publishing UK, 2019
Brockworth, Gloucestershire, England
www.blackeyespublishinguk.co.uk

ISBN: 978-1-9999583-4-3

Z D Dicks has asserted his moral right under the Copyright, Designs and Patents Act, 1988, to be identified as the author of this work.

All Rights reserved. No part of this publication may be reproduced, copied, stored in a retrieval system, or transmitted, in any form or by any means, without the prior written consent of the copyright holder, nor be otherwise circulated in any form of binding or cover other than that in which it is published and without a similar condition being imposed on the subsequent purchaser.

A CIP catalogue record for this title is available from the British Library.

Cover Picture: David Seed – Fine Artist

Cover design: Jason Conway, cre8urbrand.
                 www.cre8urbrand.co.uk

Acknowledgements to the Gloucestershire Poetry Society and its members

For Becky, Clarke and Seren

Index

23:37	7
Advice to My Younger Self	8
Ambergris	9
Apostrophe	10
Art is	11
Bed	12
City Values	13
Conker/Conquer	14
Cottage Pie	15
Crow Court	16
Crows Birthday	17
Dark Blue Cloud	18
Dementia	19
Exit Interview	20
Fee Will	21
Handwritten	22
In The Warm	23
Insomnia	24
Media Spin	25
Mosquito	26
Music	27
Ode to Arachne	28
One Small Gesture	29
Pair	30
Patriarchy	31
Pegs	32
Pioneers	33
Ritual	34
Road to Heaven	35
Silver	36
Sleepover	37
Starfish	38
Tektite	39
The Boar	40
The Doom Dog	41
The Hedgehog	42
The Mediterranean	43
The Park	44

Tiger	45
Tropical	46
Turkey-2008	47
Vermin	48
Wake	49
Words from Ted	50
Work and No Play	51

23:37

Out of the window are backs of houses
A faint sound of slow gutter-water
Outside is dry   and crystal cold

The garden grass is black
Nets dull bedroom bulbs from sight
Alternating shadows created by TV

Lamp posts turn the sky to crimson
Switch flicks amber to the right
Woman at a window sets flesh free

Downstairs comes into view
Blue kitchen glows   a cold-cut feasting fright
Half naked man tears up poultry

Squares are filled with darkness
Lazy air is the only noise at midnight
Lights extinguish   leaving low visibility

There is only black and red
There are no stars

Advice to My Younger Self

Let spiders walk into your palm
         take them outside
Never get a credit card
        be a slave
Don't buy a house
       a chain of clauses
Never get in debt
       to others' expectations

Punch harder
      everyone dies
Holidays are not an escape
If tears try
     let them leave
harden as they crystallise
Shake enemies by the hand
         but never forget
Mosquitoes bite
      spiders run
both are swatted

Ambergris

I drift in like plankton   ricochetting down a gullet
bobbing off cartilage   passing open gills
brackish water swirls up   and washes over
I settle in a crevice   as green pulses past

A bus glides with leather innards   dirt and salt in its grains
the walls are moulded metalwork   with children planted in nooks
they punt and scream   at the ocean of green   swirling by
as tiny fingers trace a scarecrow on square port holes

The whale-shark   its dorsal side   blue and black   grumbles
front open   caught prey on display   at its clear mouth   gurgling
pivoting   charging to a cloudy feeding ground   small fish overtake
with spawn in their bellies   flit away   silver sparkles disperse   the whale passes

Cars outside my window   rucksacks in footwells
kids gulp   mouths whooshing   minnows catching air
gap-toothed and strapped in
a school of four by fours ignore a red light   head into dusk

The leviathan crunches to a stop   its heart   misfiring   turning over
black steam bubbles from its vents   scorching cheeks
footfalls echo overhead   the beast convulses   a driver climbs out of his wet shadow
unfurls a tongue   a cloud of vomit trickles   like crude oil
and I'm ejected   landing in a brick net   sizzling on a street

I walk into shade   like a swimmer into the sea   submerging
away from hands that would melt together
and a meeting I could not keep   as a bus sputters its last breath

Apostrophe

Misplaced like a grocer's sign
I wait outside my home

A place where sounds can hide
my absence implied with every note

Written off by careless hands
I hover on a boundary   looking back

Cut to simplify   nowhere to go
like a key   dropped by a drunk

Exclusion marked by shirts   pancakes piled
knocking   stood in the wife's flower bed

Children say they don't need me
they will make do without

Nothing simplified   by my absence
more work to form syntax   pay bills

I can't return   close to exclamation
arms raised   to black window

A scratch on the door of the family's house
to be glossed over

Art is

        a predator scratching inside a skull
a spider eating thoughts
clawing through a body to escape

        an evacuation from a mouth
where words climb out
thick legs carrying a plump idea
ready to bite anyone   its long limbs can reach

        calloused   and blistered   fingers
hands breaching spiderlings
each scurrying   over a page   a canvas   or an instrument
laying egg sacs in eyes and ears

        an inspiration freshly laid
a beast gestating in the mind   knitting
widow tips cutting and needling
connections   clogging up mind space
until it's fully grown   unable to stay in your head
not released   it can burrow and bury itself
or worm down arteries and web up a heart

        slicing your mouth   pouring a swarm of words
when lips are matted together
over-gripping paint brushes and hatching blisters
where a blank canvas is pregnant
plucking strings   dripping afterbirth   onto a violin
as new music is born

        poking the spiders nest
ready to be infected   again

Bed

A duvet of grass   I want to climb into you
to lie   submerged   after work

Wrap myself in leaves   and hide from the sun   close my ears to noise
a passenger   drowning out a movie on an aeroplane

Beneath the insulated topsoil   I can sleep   no exhaust fumes or takeaways
a drunk   whose hangover finally fades

Bed rock will be a firm mattress   back pain numbed   muscles loosened
a constant massage by hard hands

I will close my eyes   there will be no alarm   no light   no dreams
a deep sea diver   at the limits of a pressure suit

On the frosty nights   a blanket   will keep snug   a swaddled child
like a five bar fire convecting   in a closed room

Asleep   for more than four hours a day
an insomniac finally allowed to rest

City Values

Promenade façades and dirty building backs
the shops are full of stacked clothes racks
each with three customers who have six credit cards
gentlemen wear tanned brown shoes and yachting attire
pastel fashions and overpriced socks
they carry two hundred pound satchels for sportswear
loaded with golf clubs and running shoes
that will live in a sports car
get no wear   except to share   at the bar
in men's clubs   while wives are at wine bars   mistresses wait

The city has a network of false glass fronts
where plastic is tapped on counters   pennies don't drop
art is sold in galleries   outside   buskers   sing for free
marker pen and cardboard   next to clean neon signs
performers   with portable speakers   are clapped
while citizens walk   smile   and throw shrapnel

In one window   red fake feathers hang   between adverts
of valentine wishes   pressed in Perspex   handwritten   declarations

I love my dressing gown and my sofa
and
I love my bitter Chocolates!

Each hermetically sealed   on a cut out heart   penned by one hand
outlined by crate paper   glittery string

On the cold side of a sill   a caterpillar undulates   sewing though air
a magpie lands and swallows his fill
ignores the silver sparkles   wafer wrapping   of the shop
flies home to his wife and clutch
away from the slogans and halogen fires   the gridlock of slick cars
and the exhausted cold city

Conker/Conquer

I used to like conkers   but the spiders went away
no running shadows in front of the fireplace
no climbing beasts under the sofa
no fear the floor was made of something worse than lava

What scared me   was my grandmother's rug   faux fur and brown stripes
each clump   a ball of legs that would wake up and detach
when I dozed in the rippling orange   of five glowing bars
my eyes would scan carpet valleys for a pattern in black

But conkers were placed in dying summer days
balancing on sills   tables and sideboards
webs greyed and clumped with dust
abandoned windows had no nets

The horseflies snuck in   one landed on my bare wrist
its scalpel cut a ravine that dripped down fingers
milk teeth clamped   needles dug for purchase   ripping skin
my left hand swiped   dragging needles down   smearing a mix of fluid

I asked for closed shutters and watched the ceilings
I lifted boxes   cleared clutter and conkers sunk in drains
flies tore up curtains   buzzing into crocheted silk
the spiders nestled in the cosy hair rug   and I never got bitten again

Cottage Pie

At the corner of a holiday chalet
a cottage pie congeals against glass
bubbling steam and evacuating stock
misting   it permeates the membranes of nostrils

A copy   an imitation   or   a tribute to Escher
is printed in black and white   on loose trousers
it rests on hips and sinks   into her horizontal cleft
cutlery skids across an unpacked   erected   flatpack table
permanently bolted to a carpet
smooth fingers spread and flatten   over a placed spoon
a magazine sits low on a seat   an oval expands and underwear stretches
tendons tighten as a body folds at the waist
pictures of models are picked up   folded and thrown
shoulder straps twist down a soft bicep   exposing a sprung breast

A pendulum of rump sways in the kitchen
succulent   tender and relaxed
a delicacy is placed down   two words are cooed
dig in
saliva pools on a tongue   saline solution oozes from meat
black ink bleeds in eyes   hot flesh buries inside a warm hole
filling a throat
knives and forks are placed in parallel
one question is asked   and a manicured eyebrow arches
What is for pudding?

Crow Court

Judge Crow marched past rooks
cawed on his lofty stump   knocking for order
the jury in black suits   already seated
Magpie entered the dock leaves   to answer for grand theft
on a trimmed patch   in front of Judge Crow

Barrister Raven didn't call for witnesses
to keep Magpie grounded and doing bird
a mass of black cloaks
deposited silver   in front of jailbird feathers
he wasn't permitted to touch exhibits
the forty at his feet

Magpie was the only one with a stripy suit
they sang loudly it wasn't about race
just the crimes committed   thieving
from nests to make ends meet   sew a nursery
the defendant lowered his head
his beak marks over metal

The verdict fell as a conker hit roots
the crows would come and strip his nest
Magpie would be homeless
stuck foraging   with pigeons
rebranded rock-doves

The Jury in black   and the Judge above
glistened with wealth and leg-tags
Magpie shook his head   flash-dazzled wings
flew and fled   one for sorrow
a buzzard saw a shimmer   but Magpie was gone
exhibits   one to forty   in his claws
leaving the court to adjourn   scramble for trees

Crows Birthday

A crows tongue flaps out   a foil party horn   celebrating death
in the gutter lies a tramp   a piñata   of rags
the corvid ceased cheering   snapped his beak   spied a soft spot of cloth
bobbing forward   cocking head   he aims for a finger   a party sausage
oozes out syrup   jam from a roll   open eyes don't watch him eat

There is only cartilage on a hand   that once cut cake
dusted crumbs   from a sticky slice   almond and marzipan
feathers flexing   he serenades himself   makes a wish
his friends arrive   for a piece

They will pop eyes   balloons on strings
pick holes in a belly   like digits in jelly
engorge   on gift wrapped treats   as a hollow man spills insides
ignore tablets laying on grit   next to a bottle
eat their fill of buffet food   fly off with painted faces
take away party bags   share spoils with families

Dark Blue Cloud

Judge Crow chatters on a black branch   a baby cries
The sky   powdered white   is blotted with grey and navy
Swirling shelf clouds   electrically   charge oxygen   sweet and zingy
The jury scatter to rooftops   following a path of blood

A tortoise shell mongrel   lands heavily on scruffy paws   with a clamped jaw
Lungs   weighted with mucus   strain in duvet heat   breathing by a bush
Pulses rustle flecks of white fur   and a single cold sphere   hits   a clammy forehead
Covering the garden   shadows chill skin   in a coat of congealed sweat

The young chick has stopped crying   there are no songs
Yellow grass   the soil bald and split   the sun has killed it
Powdered ash thickens   into gravy brown   granules expand and merge in wet

On a slab   in growing pitch   a mucky eater raises its chin   flickering lights
Concrete   stained red   meat runs   jelly solidifies
A beak points up and a drop lands in an eye
Forks interrupt dinner   rain   a murder has been spotted

Dementia

A paper thin hand of bone and blue skin   grips a pen
scrawling a title   black ink digging   embossing a page

> *Important things to remember*
> *Bananas are a good source of potassium*

At a desk a woman wiggles her feet   in pressure socks
moulded around ankles   earth around roots
she holds a fountain pen lid in her lips   and wheezes
a bonfire crackle

> *Bananas   a good source of potassium*
> *My daughter's name is June*

A memory rises   cut stump growing   past the weeds
and long grass   keeping it in darkness
the day a baby was born   and the agony of shedding fruit   as she grew

> *Bananas are high in potassium*
> *I garden pot plants*

Workmen   in goggles and mouth masks   saw   slicing an old tree
teeth blades score across a ringed base   like plaque in a brain   cutting connections

> *Bananas   high in potassium*
> *Husband is dead*

A blank space where a life used to be   an oak
felled out of existence   wood chip and scattered branches
lose colour   greenery growing around a base   of a family tree
rent   out of shape

> *Bananas are potassium*
> *My name is*
> *Bananas*

Exit Interview

What Did You Dislike Most About Your Job?
What Did You Like Most About Your Job?
Why Are You Leaving Your Current Position?

Glass sealed in 1st story office   plastic   a sympathetic smile
the crack den   over the road   spilling   a battering ram   sharp stick
splintered deep into the entrance   an ants nest of junkies   scamper to kerb
eye contact relegated   a flat hand scuffs paper   across the stained desk

The last question hung   a spider spinning before a grinning toad
fresh suit   blue tie   a uniform for a ritual
trousers steamed   cuffs folded   jacket on back of chair
part undressed   sweating in a fanless room

Finger tips stretch and tap their twins   heels bounce   under a chair   as floral perfume sweats
from a half painted jawline   assistant manager picking up envelope   scratching
glossed nails   into folds   hands rest on bobbing knees   lungs sinking a full breath   sirens
fading through clear walls   legs settling   palms dried   a furrow appearing over caked wrinkles

An open window   to be closed by a hand   or shouting   to be jumped from
the whole of your family   could be   mangled by fuselage   in a cars crumple zones
inhaling black coffee   five mornings a week   stale body odour   guarding a mug
hitting KPI's   promotions   going to fish lipped   part timers   watching tea stagnate

Fee Will

A cockroach crawls from a vent   flutters caramel
down to paper   fist-smashed   on contract   chitin spread like junk
and a man stares into polished glass   tie choking   dusts shoulders
grabs a smeared remnant   opens door

He slaps leather satchel on roof   car pulls out and sheets spread   twist in rain
curl   flatten   washed grey to gutter   wheels cut puddles
brakes whinny   stopping   in glossed lines   water drumming chassis
a soggy suit enters foyer   stairs echo   black shoes patter up shaft

A conference room   stormed   and an audience   remain   seated
hands   tap trouser pockets   scramble up chest   a sleep walker waking
naked   he clears throat   one weighty breath   pulled through teeth
fingers cross behind jacket   *The last will and testament reads:*

Handwritten

The essay was placed on the desk
black ink   scratched in waves   floating and sinking
dragged and smeared   over lined horizons

A web of blotched sentences   matted across paper
spindly exoskeletons   weaved into words
sharpening to points

It looks like a spider has scrawled across your page, stop joining up.

Crosses littered the page   like Jesus at his execution
the marker crucifying errors

These are the words of a madman!

Thick claret circles   arrow wound   a snake though paragraphs
the page embossed by notes   that merged   with fountain nib dribble
worm writhing down the margin
a single correction   repeated   sinking in the holes of the essay
with the occasion comment

Really?!
Is this relevant, the register is off and the imagery makes no sense.

A wound in the paper   at the t of relevant
the blast from a magnum   a disposable pen   had cauterised instantly
but dried blood remained   on the body   of the text

The page was flipped   at the bottom   a paragraph   written in red capitals
the Head of English finished

Too Many Speling mistakes.

A coffee ring   stamped as a signature

In the Warm

The snow used to tickle my nose
smell like wet wood and frozen grass
now   it whispers in my ears
and swirls at my face   biting my eyes
soon   it will be moulded by a smile
as my children make sculptures   with carrot and coal faces
launching fiery missiles

The wind used to caress my cheeks
and cool the sun on my closed lids
now   it cuts me and splits my hands
drying and stripping   wrinkling skin
soon   the breeze will chill my lungs
and make me cough ash
in puffs of steam

The cold was a clean wash
that rinsed my pores and clothes
now   it's my reason to go outside
the birds sing to me in their skeletal nooks
one day   I will hide behind glass
watch my children   throwing compact missiles
at bobble headed infants

Insomnia

Outside   in the deepest silences of night
I flip a phone on and off   no messages
tobacco mist shares its drug   with kitchen light   passed the back door
a dull headache   lulled by beer   air is hazed by bitter sugar breath
dredging memories in a sea sick ship
of coming horizons   ports abandoned
where somber yellow   booming whispers   swirl and storm in a head

A glow crackles   blue smoke twists to bushes
last dregs of lungs   hiss to mist
the sun will thaw bones
break nicotine hues   that intrude   twirl in wet webs
send a toad   groaning   croaking   crashing in dark mulch

No quiet   while a maelstrom roars   in silent ears
a stick is toked   bridge of a nose   squeezed
no turning off flashes of summer smiles   an unscented neck
held close   only   hours ago   the patio is grey   grass is black
no house makes noise
there are no bird songs   beyond the kitchen door
no animals   no burglars

Only muted clouds   no
rain   warmed hand   lighter in pocket   patter from the drain
no smell in tight nostrils   nothing
to wash away   a duvet of clammy skin   no
kiss to sign off the day

Media Spin

Over concrete buildings   a feather tail looped   rolled
Dizzying down   along stores   TV screens merging
Crow span   through a hot current
The barracuda swam   in thick mulch

The earth in the clouds and Crow grounded in air

The sea gull trampled   along a web
A spider danced   over tree tops

A black meteor arced   tumbling and sinking in blue

The monkey cartwheeled   into a chip shop
And a man sauntered forward   his tusks smashing a tree

Crow fell faster and animals twisted in high definition

The hippo charged   to catch a fly
A frog lunged   to bite a seal

 Shops muffled programmes in glass

The whale clenched its mouth of blades   to open a tin of beans
The woman twisted a handle   smashing a termite hive

 Pedestrians dropped bags   pointing to a corvid cannon ball

The aardvark dug   inside a pack of sweets
A toddler rustled   and his beak twitched

The winged pebble plunged   piercing leaves
Hacking through twigs   Crow   lowered his head
His shadow indented snow
Credits rolled   and lights went out

Mosquito

A helicopter drone of wings   hovers
    to a landing pad of hair   skin
chop   from a flitting hand   swerved
    skids dust down   pump connects   a tank refuels
fingers scratch   a no fly zone
    mortar fire   palms slap
brush   across occupied ground
    goggle eyes brace to ditch   avoid a missile strike
spinning   at low altitude
    listing   to bush
barrel rolling   engines judder
    a swerving retreat
into pitch   bomb sites swell
    nails scrape
sun tanned shoulders
    itch

Music

A spider in bathroom sits on a rail   meshing and looping
the purple shower curtain   to the towels
spinning on a current   pirouetting to a lake
from a soft frame   flecked with green   glossed white   matted with fog
to the top of a tub   and a tile seam

A man stares in the mirror   grey sockets spreading
peering at bird feet   cross stitched
weaved and stretched down cheeks   pouring   onto barren shores
bottom eyelid fingered down   vessels raised   a tapestry of forking rivers

The false widow shakes off   her old brown dress
white virgin again   soft in warm haze   body spreading   tip toes floating
a gymnast hanging   from a ribbon   needles plucking through steam
dancing   until her new outfit dries out

A river in the shower meanders
sponge sinking down   his dead reef body   stripping flora   from skin-bed
exploring and dredging trenches   foam filling cavities
a pulsing tide washes away remnants   deepening creases in his suit

A speaker   on a stained shelf   curls words to mist
colour is spun into a new dress   marked by noisy yellow
feet two step over a tub bank   hardening   callous
pale   on a frayed course towel   drying in a warm song
cracking with static

Ode to Arachne

Lustrous black hangs over pale skin
Gleaming green under deities sight
Wheeling toes transfer lanolin
Watchers skill shadows this neophyte
Who's damning dexterity draws in
The old woman watching weaving
Whispering advice to halt spokes
But fibrous boasts offend mountain
War horns sound an electric warning
Arachne's eyes roll with faster strokes

Athena whets sharp javelin
Circling pressure spills lymphocyte
An emerald eyed grimalkin
Issues a challenge instead of a fight
To save face in front of her kin
Anxiously she begins fabricating
Charring wood, wisping smoke
Arachne remembers old sin
Clean fingers start recording
Twenty one episodes to provoke

Woven lust impregnates linen
Details capture a birthright
Divine lashes flicker, flecking venin
Mortal legs levitate, threads snap and choke
Defiant victory from the coffin
Punished and reborn with aconite
To appease her guilt for a relaxed reign
Arachne is transformed and hanging
Always spinning; a masterstroke

One Small Gesture

On a red playhouse roof   snails sup the last dregs of rain
three molluscs slowly bake   scramble in their cooking pot homes
tracing reservoirs   tucked in creases   hot plastic water   not yet smoke
stinking   of methamphetamine   bubbling and warping

A man's digits pluck   unsealing   lifting slime   by speckled shells
dropping to plant pot   a wife's favourite   onto dark mulch
snails wiggle   retract eye stalks   spread their feet   nuzzling deep
in turgid leaves   petrol rainbows over webs

A rolled cigarette   withered by heat   is crushed   leaking menthol wisps   to shade
bare feet press stones   a man grasps   clunks shut his door   plants into sofa
bastes in shorts   his eyelids fall   juddering   head lolls
butterflies hide   seagulls   drunk on ants   peck windscreens   and clouds bleed black

The man clambers to the garden   molluscs gone
a crow stabs at shards   raises its chest   cackles   shoots over trees   into a field   croaks
falls and flattens   onto uncut crops   on a bed of nails
flies gnaw out feathers   writhing larvae pop like blisters   and the harvest grows

Bluebottles disperse   like firework frazzle   sizzling embers   dance to soil
their plump bodies   water bombs   impact in cracks   and burst
under charred bird   damp leaks   bleeding rich umber   closing split earth
a farmer threshes   slicing a husk   and churns in a mill

Brake discs screech and a baker signs   he slams down a sack
kneads and cooks   wraps bread   to be sold in shops   a wife buys a paper and a loaf
painted fingers press down a timer   tap   click   knife smears   gold sinks
the man eats in the garden   watches snails   climbing into the wife's plant pot

Pair

The moon half lights the dusted black sky   in burning chill

Two magpies spread finger-feathers   and glide onto a skeletal aerial

A frog piggy-backed by her husband   sloppily springboards   through damp grass
like a hippo on a pogo stick

A spider tip-toes through drops of glue   to wake up his wife   playing silk
a harpist   serenading   at a funeral

A dragonfly bends its tail   fusing plates with a partner
like children's digits   forming a segmented heart

A mongrel launches onto a purebreds back   pumping and bone-locking
like an arm caught in a fence

A cat mews on a barbed tom   singing into a thorny bush
a banshee who couldn't be saved

A man calls to his lady   joining her arm-in-arm
chain clicking   sealed

The moon flinches and flickers
with a passing streak   of sparking shreds

Multi-coloured powders ignite   fireworks clap   echoes boom
molten blasts shake glass   in red brick houses

Two birds in their glittering   nestle down

Shoulders   nuzzled   in steaming cold
the man and his lady   message when home
sweat   in single beds

Patriarchy

I stand over the oven   tablet screen flickering
a woman screams
purple placard disturbed   by wind

Eight out of ten women do more housework

I open a packet   children on sofa
testing springs   tomatoes slung

Splash-back sprays from chrome
flesh   diced   speaker shakes case

Women earn less than men!

I pick a clean finger   press
down volume   son   daughter
snatch and bicker   laying table

Bolognese bubbles   plates placed

We're tired of   mansplaining

I call my offspring   to their high
backed seats   screen turns black
carry steaming sauce   serve

Pegs

On the kitchen top is a black peg bag
next to the oven   is a steel jawed   plastic   crocodile
in the cupboard   a bread bag is pinched at the neck
a wooden gripper   sealing it
next to the drainer   a grey one leaks water   from its closed mouth   unable to soak up water

The pegs used to be in a ripped zip bag   with a hook   on the line
a tepid gust   sometimes   spat over its teeth   through the cargo   stirring and clicking
the sack belly bulged   dribbled an odd pincher   where it fell into a rug of grass
earth filled crannies   the lost were buried   smelling of musky leaves
they were washed with downpours and bleached   in cloudless pink skies

Soon   the pegs will be under my mattress   to hold on a loose bedspread
they will be on clothes   pinning small school jumpers   to radiators   pooling onto laminate
tucked away in carrier bags   a stash of spares   on a hook   under the stairs
in my back pack   just in case I need them at work   where there may   one day   be no coat stand
they will be on me if I'm cut   holding my skin together   or   pulling TV wires away from the fire

On the kitchen top   the peg bag is flat   an eyeless sunken fish
the baby crocs   that lived inside   have been released   to gobble up the house
every day a new spawn appears   gnawing   placed by a woman
keeping the house fresh   secure and sealed   one peg at a time
I am disorganised
She's got me pegged

Pioneers

A stream chills rocks   salmon sleep   in their nooks
      manicured feet   in slippers

At a frosty bank   a beaver   hacks at wood
      a flannel shirted man
loading a flatbed   stump graves   marking fallen

In a white clearing   a caribou sheds velvet   nibbles blueberries
      a gladiator lounging   after sparring

At a cabin   two men bark   point
                              a foot marks a line   in snow

one throws a hat   with a built-in torch   faces flush and brows rise
shouts bounce   from an audience of trees
      like a police cordon at a street fight

Contracts are drawn   at ten paces   spread on a desk   splintered redwood
gloved hands pause   reach   connect

A polar bear erupts from the trees   the salmon sleeps in its nook
beaver   on its back   floating   caribou   lounges   eating
and two loggers run   plans abandoned

Ritual

Keys rustle   fourteen hours   since   last at home
the front door booms shut   and shoes skid off
cool air   curtains wave   as a bag thumps   sofa leather
a question asked   nod   grunts reply   and naked feet patter   to kitchen

white zip pulled   and a uniform collapses   wire bra   unhooked
warm nipples harden   a kettle rumbles   coughs   click
surface echoes   as glass lands heavy   sugar jar spooned   bottle tipped
                                                        drip rolls   down mug

evaporating   hips jiggle   mug in hand   fingers numb at rim
outstretched   offering handle

screen clunked on   soap   mind-washes   grime of the day   curl up   sticking to seat
cuddled   with a sweet treat
                              drinking
                                    dozing
                                          melting
rinse   repeat

Road to Heaven

Vapour sears skin   hissing from a spring
stale urea fills the air   where carcasses leak   stinking of copper and beef
strapped   silhouette walls   faces are layered in rust
metal   pressed in   charred crust shells   weeping burgundy tears
throats shred from overuse
the air   thick with rumbles

Below   an orange glow casts a shadow   above
naked rock   dusted by a film of dry blood
sharp outcrops dig in feet   hopping   from flat to crevice
tiny embers flicker   flies   burning out
each kiss   sizzles into a galaxy of sores
the sky is a cloud   silent fireworks pop   blisters   raining white smoke

The scarred dead shamble   blind
their forms withered   ash cloud statues
others swarm   unable to feel   in crocodile scales
they scrape past each other   sealed mouths   eyes crack
no flesh   just salt and steam
bleeding sparks on manmade magma
wisps are sucked   sputtered by scorched lungs
in the fallout   civilians wander in the ochre darkness   alone in their trillions

Silver

Magpie saw white pain   in the left side   of his skull
like a wave of brain freeze   a lustrous blade   through a socket
he paused   wings behind back   beak down   head cocked
wincing palms shaded foreheads
a   would-be   prince addressed pedestrians
from a precious podium   eyeing a ten pence piece

A Zimmer frame rattles   on grey   rubber   knobs
outside a bingo hall   a woman in   slip-on   beige shoes
drills   stubbing   lipsticked tip   in thick   slack tights
shuffling trunks   in a wide turning circle   nudging
scratching cupronickel on a kerb   hanging halfway over a drain

Magpie performs last checks   on steering assembly
stabilises spoilers   a yin-yang   cannon ball from a tree
like a roller coaster in free-fall
thrusters taper up   as he arcs on a current
like a jet pack pulsing
feather rudders flex   to a hover   boosters extinguish
above a   weed-walled   grey slab
black landing columns brace   thud
scurrying for cover   rolling into a bush   robber mask pokes out

Dazzle camouflage   from shade   skipping past butts
range four metres and closing   combat flapping over a can
a pink skateboard stops   by an open gutter   small hand reaches
plastic watch   grinning kitten clock face   shakes its head
Magpie pecks a paw
coin flips up
like a mirror at sea
and dunks

Sleepover

Trees sprinkle the scent of almond and chestnut
the night is coming and the sky is white
a pulsing gust used to growl with cars   rubber kicking up tarmac
skateboards and roller skates   children's feet echoed on brick
the path outside   cools with taps   puddles growing   splitting with ice

The horizon glows   soft ember crumbling
a cat traces a gull   as it squawks to nest
stomachs gurgled   like washing machines   filled with shoes
kitchen full with   left over   carrot and cabbage
ghosts of roast beef steam   wafts   from an outlet pipe
mother slowly fans eyelids   in front of screen
and a dog shivers   set free   out of the back door

Mango and pink swirl though clouds
a chimney coughs   plumes   blue   black
bees dab at bushes   pigeons pull at branches
bed time stories will be read
and   I   won't be home tonight

Starfish

A starfish   faceless and often unseen
except by those   who dredge it up   people fishing
when it's hoisted   it twists and dries
in salty air   it dies

A starfish should be left to crawl   in a sea of privacy
not picked apart by strangers hands   feeling rough skin
drained   skeletal   no buoyancy
submerged   we heal lost limbs   sightless   with no urgency

Sometimes we get unstuck   drawn by a hook
lifted and inspected   our union is rejected
so   we
          drop
shrouded in a blanket of waves
                                      we sink like lost doubloons
where snares can't touch us

Tektite

I feel a rough dark egg
pocked with cavities   heavy glass
turn it in my hand   wrap in paper

A meteor spun   blasted by cosmic rays   suspended in nothing
past super novas and black holes   through ice rings
ricocheting   off moons   fractured by glancing hits   a misshapen pinball
as nebulas grew and died   basking stars soaked up umbra   the block hurtled on
catapulted around the sun   a game of dodgems
narrowly   missing bumpers   exospheres scuffing rock
circling solar system   our neighbourhood
building momentum for its kamikaze raid   the first of us   looking to a burning night
where a tail bent   crackling   thumping to our planet's side
melting   tectonic skin   spraying liquid to the moon
a blending of bodies   ebon tears   globular rain   cooled
in stratosphere   ink stones of a thunder god   buried like shrapnel into earth

I rotate the scarred surface   strum thumb over ripples
pocket it   for my son

The Boar
(Population control)

Through wet woodland
growling hunters slog on empty stomachs
wellies scrunch and squelch
yomping after cloven prints   shotguns hanging low
like unused hiking sticks

Non-native pigs   *illegally*   roam in streets
feral farm-bred boar
mixed-race sows with large sounders
prompt twitchy net-curtains
while husbands sweat and snore

Boots slide on a drop kerb
onto reflective tarmac
sticks and stones   are lodged   in hard cold teeth
thick brown   stodge   clumped with green bristles
is unpicked and stomped
littering   like earthen breadcrumbs   to a store

In the local shop   dragging yellow leaves
a hybrid knocks over cereals and baskets
snuffling and lifting blind eyes
butting a pensioner and busting a knee
razor tusks   claret   and covered in faeces

A hunter after a pack of crisps   whistles
he dings through automatic doors
sucking in warm air and closing an eye
his barrel rises   trigger-pull scatters shot
bloodied old man spread on the floor
in a quilt of black pudding and bacon
snorts like a pig

The Doom Dog

              has sable claws   polished like spider fangs
oily fur   matted and heavy   it climbs on me when I sleep
its silent weight spreads on my chest
a wide mouth and needle teeth
claret eyes   that glow   like bloody lights
It makes no sound

I'm a block   in bed
the clotheshorse fluttering   by the curtained window
washing wafts   like a tropical beach after a storm
a large mirror rests on the floor   sunken in carpet
leaning on the wardrobe   glass facing the wall
to stop shadows   getting out

Its low head appears   under the door handle
faint yellow from the landing   coats its fur in flames
vinegar-stung eyelids   collapse   and I'm planted
rib cage crushed and gut punched
my face opens to   swirling grease and sweat
the dog turns to smoke   its soot sinking into my throat

It twists   gnawing and knotting   tightening shoulders
I sit up   a headstone at a grave   and stand   eyes frozen open
the grey room   spins   when I stagger
I search for a door   that isn't there   as air strokes wet skin
pulling at a scalp   to escape   the demon inside
the beast that hollows out my chest   plunges to intestines
blackens the world   a heart misfire   and reminds me   I will die

The Hedgehog

A fortress of spikes and wet earth   like brambles after rain
snuffles in soil   tip toeing   in black
it trudges on concrete and grass   over front lawns and roads
engine pistons and dump valves hiss   under lamplight
flashes and oily chassis dash overhead   as it meanders past flat frogs and leaking dead

It used to sleep   eyes unpeeling
when   screaming   children poked spiky sides
never shuffling along painted lines   or   eating from shiny bowls
curled in bush blanket   where predators couldn't smell
only waking after winter

Pink feet trundle   past signs   white arrows smeared with grime
spines turned grey   volcano ash victim   a snout sneeze through exhaust
rotten eggs spew from tubes   scalding skin
cars pull off from queues   a hedgehog goes back to dirt

The Mediterranean

Workers walk from tin roof houses
single floored   low cobweb wires
trail over   narrow roads

Sparkling blue   trimmed palm trees   walled off cliffs   little England
the block hotel shadows a road in morning   shields pools in afternoon
grill steam mingled with chlorine   tan lines cover swimmers   ghosts of swimsuits
a clear bottomed boat drifts   engine frothing   mast naked   a hollow fin

Spanish love songs   mingle with guitar plucking   doesn't mask
children splashing   blasting   double barrels   pumping pistols   in a goggled war
there are no birds   save   black bird   dark thrush   and a pigeon   who
joins a buffet line   picking at cereals   bees meander through lavender   hungry tourists

A mosquito   lands on a bug-sprayed face   false lashes of legs   ignorant
of brand guarantees   nuzzling   before being swiped
a security man   in black cap and shorts   adjusts cream compression socks   pushing baton around
belly   an elderly father sparks   behind a bush   no line of sight   two minute family reprieve

Violet sunset   half cut queens   English accents sing   from sunburnt breasts
stunted pirates   jig   under   painted   paper hats   shirtless men flex
and sway   sucking in guts   swash bucklers   preteens   disappear to quarters
a glass clatters   shattering   the coming tide   dispersing on rocks   warmed by gust and cheer

The bar closes   hospitality staff chatter over street
mouths wrinkled from smiling in sun
shadows lengthen lines

The Park

A dog prances with a red ball   man thumb flicks phone
the dog   on two legs   waiting
to fetch   prams circle a blanket   baby bobs on crossed legs

Tops of trees flutter   bell rings   around
terrier's neck   cocks at the base of a statue   stood smiling   stone wrinkles rained away
skateboarder pads past puddle   foot strumming path   parallel to parked cars

Tent-worn   patches   a pigeon glides over
facing tennis players   who bend at waists   smash balls
on court   rattling shots onto a cage   ruffling rosemary   in its bed

One cloud dulling the sun   a white plane groans   in clear sea above
shade   onto mismatched benches   embossed by sentences   *In memory of a loving mother*
clunking over curb   scratched   spattered by paint   a van edges toward them

Motorbike echo   roaring from walls   petrol fug   screeches   rubber smoke
gusting pollen   across bark and over leaves   into puffy faces
under a drone   scattered   behind a building   topped by a painted lion

Elderly scuff through short grass   hands shield glasses
birds chirrup   coo   from an unknown tree
straining to push peddles   a toddler   tests stabilisers

Chains creak   squeak   father pushes two swings   a lazy boxer striking
wheels slow   scraped by trainers   like scuba shoes   neon cyclist   clicks to gate
sweating in a cap   a traffic warden   wipes his forehead   with back of hand

Children calling   their clothes dry brushed   by stains   and brown dust
waving   dismissed with fingers   parents under parasols   drink cheap coffee
a man lies on his back   bag for a pillow   doesn't see anything

Tiger

Crusty knuckles rubbed eye crumbs and flexed
fingers stretching   to mash a snooze switch
a slipper slumbers under the bed
while keys hibernate down the back of a sofa
and glasses nestle   on top of the fridge

Cold carpet indents skin
toast pops and butter's thickly basted
white tops are pulled onto children and teeth pasted
a course brush combs though knots
tights are pulled up and a cardigan buttoned

The shower head dribbles and a faucet runs dust
but a parent needs scrubbing
a full kettle   takes three minutes to boil
and the warm tap   from the sink   can fill a bowl in four
washing   before the sprint   will take five
heart drumming ribs on lungs   six minutes to get to school

Boots jerk open   socks slip in   and a door slams closed
hair steams a smoke-cloud   that condenses down a back
jacket unzipped and pulled over shoulders
infant hands softly dragged   tiptoe-dashing
two minutes until classrooms close   or
fifteen minutes to queue   at the front desk   and get a red mark

At the end of the road   a tiger waits for breakfast
breathing slows and little feet plant
school lessons will begin   an office will open
a wristwatch moves   but   the numbers blur
a threat is free and time has stopped
there is a tiger at the crossroad   and it can't be ignored

Tropical

Air wafts   the scent of pink lotus flowers

                                        no rubbish on a shoreline

your lips taste of sweet fruit and blue water

a smooth swimmer   stretching out in a pool

                                        not a tourist   yelling at a guide

a single malt whiskey   clinking with cold rocks

the soft boom of drums and a rustling skirt

                                        not a crow   walking streets   stinking of meat

you'll be   a naked washed beach

warm water over my feet   caressing in waves

                                        not poison exhaust in my throat

you'll be the sizzling pink   of a thin steak

crinkled pages on fingers

                                        not clammy skin   in a draught

you'll be the sun   soaking into closed lids

Turkey-2008

Along sandy pavements   outstretched hands   circled us closer
dark eyes   shadowed   by thick brows   widened at your hair
one street seller asked   *How much?   How much?*
I put an arm around your shoulder   we kept walking

Turkey was a sausage factory   the beach was laden
pork bellies churned   charred chipolatas hung   smoked in salt air
while you hid behind shades   drank cocktails   ignoring trade offers for camels

I take you to dinner   you looked at baubles outside shops
Everything is bartered here   never accept the price
into a flat roofed restaurant   we slipped
through beads   coffee spun with smoke
you ordered steak and spiced rice   no pork   only fake bacon

We sashayed through the alfresco charcuterie   to our hotel
where the maids were male

Vermin

Glass needles crown the high-street bank   façade
multi-storey car park   meshed   in anti-suicide wires
pigeons mumble   grounded   on path
anti-ram raiding pillars   occasional   resting spots
glossed black bollards of street teeth
sprayed   with viscous white
entrances invaded   by flying rats

Desiccated bench   has rows of arm rests
a homeless man   dread-locks   pink bandana
and tan slipper-boots   hits
a seat   with a faded bergen
no space to lodge   his luggage

Department store   next to automatic door
pigeons land   and stumble   on stone pyramids
that line concrete walls   digging in   to those that sit

Grey sky turning black
thin legs stagger   under a rumbling bridge
wet shoulders slump   dirty face looks down
tightly packed   cement spikes   line the unused underpass

The pigeons retreat to the park   sparse trees   cut short
canopies hide squirrels and bats   birds settle in tops
no space on dry stumps
a tramp sits   on a spineless   damp bench
elbows on thighs   chin on hands

His hat sat on path
no change

Wake

My cross-hatching waves   shimmer
at your passing   froth flung   moved by absence
glittery skin   a million stars   rained
into the sea   pulsing green   cool   under your bow   I'm broken
to hold you   cut   by your bladed body   I swirl inside
but you would sail over   and away

My lover washed up   sails abandoned   to die
                                          relinquish wetness
                                                              crack in rust
                                                                                     crumble on land
leaving me to crash   against rocks
                                    alone
                                                pulled to earth
                                                              at night
the tide stretching to join us
                                    one last time

Words from Ted
Husband, Father and Grandfather

I remember when the Graf Spee was sunk   it was when I hid my cigarettes
down a rabbit hole   so I wouldn't get caught by my parents   and the next day
they were soaked   I stopped hunting not long after   animals shouldn't suffer
Do you want me to cook you a bacon sandwich   and a few fried chips?
Did you turn the freezer off?   It's gone to pot   fancy a *choc ice*?   When two lines appear
on the back of your neck   your   elevenses are up   A man should only live
four score year and ten   Never trust a man   whose shoes are worn
on the inside of their feet   Trust your instincts   Never trust united artists   Trust me
The way the world is going   it's going to go backward   Science fiction is just fantasy
Always remember the difference   between direct and alternating current   If I
were your father   I   would give you the taste of my belt   sometimes   You never change
Travel the world   when you're young   it's easier   I wanted to go   to Africa
and do some good   but   the doctors wouldn't let me   You can do anything
you're more clever than me   Do you need   something to eat   some money   a lift?
Life is all an illusion   you get it now   this is my first time   in hospital   they've treated me well
Well   there you go   I'll see you tomorrow   *and I didn't*

Work and No Play

Magpie sifts through undergrowth   spies a berry
a black-beaked raven barks   and grabs a stalk
escaping to clean air
a tight shirted drunk
crow-bars out of a crowded bar   belching birds into flight
taking his pint   out to a beer garden

Magpie scurries across a flat top roof
a lady-bird lands on a ledge
like a jumbo jet checking outboard flaps
it scuttles into a shadow

A sparrow touches down probing with its pincers
like chopsticks pushing through rice
into a crack in felt
squeezing and pulling out a dumpling
it unearths a shell and twitchy legs

Magpie touches down to silt
wading by a pond
seeds are scattered onto a bank
he runs with wings out   a mallard slaps   and bobs
his flat billed-beak hoovers   in mud creases
a greedy leaf blower with a clown horn

Magpie sees a nest and eggs
parent birds out stealing food
he nuzzles down and sets a place
home in time for dinner

www.ingramcontent.com/pod-product-compliance
Lightning Source LLC
Chambersburg PA
CBHW081433070526
44586CB00020B/2567